THE PATH OF TRUE HEALING

10-Step Process "From Pain to Power."

By
Marquis Dorsey

COPYRIGHT @ 2023 THE PATH OF TRUE HEALING
By Marquis Dorsey

ISBN:
Hardbound-978-621-470-766-9
Softbound/Paperback-978-621-470-767-6
PDF (downloadable)-978-621-470-768-3

Published by:
Poetry Planet Book Publishing House
Rosario, Pozorrubio, Pangasinan, Philippines Contact Number: 09554960094
Email: maritesritumalta@gmail.com

DEDICATION

This book is dedicated to people who are screaming in Silence. I am with you.

I will help you gain your power back, your strength, and your faith in yourself back.

I will help you identify the problem step by step, and you will be able to overcome everything that made you lose your power.

I want you to face things you had a fear of and take the power it had over you back.

This is your life, and in 10 steps, we will end this process with our heads up with no more pain and all of our power.

Author's Note

Many of us may identify with the road to recovery. Each of us faces our unique challenges and hardships. Some of us have it far more complex than others, and we must scrap and claw our way through life. How I went from being a crack baby to a successful businessman is the subject of this memoir.

It wasn't easy being a crack baby growing up. Due to my mother's drug abuse, I spent most of my youth moving in with various relatives and acquaintances. I suffered a lot of emotional stress since I never felt accepted by anyone. After years of avoiding dealing with my issues, I finally began to progress toward recovery when I forced myself to confront the anxiety and sadness that had plagued me for so long.

On my path, I discovered how crucial it was to ask myself these questions: For whom am I fighting? What am I fighting for? Am I even ready to fight? Thinking about everything we must overcome can leave us feeling overwhelmed and frustrated. But when we breathe and remember why we're fighting, we find the strength to keep going.

It's crucial to know our vulnerabilities and talents while we're up against our inner demons. The enemy here is not an external foe but our traumatic experiences and identities. It's not simple to face the problems that have plagued us for years, but knowing our capabilities and limitations better equips us to battle them.

True healing is a complicated process that should not be rushed. Before the battle even begins, we must be prepared to do it alone. You'll need a lot of grit and perseverance to pull this out. It's not enough to hope for a better world. It's something we have to seek out and work for consciously.

On my road to recovery, I discovered something crucial: I can't beat this thing if I have no idea what or who I'm up against. Understanding the impact of my trauma on my life was something I needed to devote some time to. Because of this, I could face my problems head-on and find solutions to them.

My life had almost insurmountable obstacles, yet I overcame them all and found success thanks to the advice and inspiration in this book. It's proof that, with effort, we can overcome anything and achieve true healing. This is not a simple path, but it is one worth taking.

I wrote this book in the hopes that it will encourage those going through tough times. When things appear bleak, I want people to know that there is a light at the end of the tunnel. Everyone has the potential for deep healing and the discovery of inner strength. I pray that my life's experience will encourage and inspire anyone who reads it.

PREFACE

Because of the multifaceted nature of healing, which includes both the body and the mind, a holistic strategy is typically necessary for lasting improvement. True healing is rarely quick or straightforward, but it is always worthwhile. My own life and studies have taught me that the first step toward recovery is to accept and embrace our brokenness. In my book, "The Path of True Healing: From Pain to Power," I provide guidance and resources for developing emotional maturity, self-awareness, and the ability to bounce back from adversity.

"Vulnerability is the birthplace of innovation, creativity, and change" (Brown, 2010) is a quote from Dr. Brené Brown, a prominent researcher on vulnerability and shame. By being honest about our weaknesses and hurt feelings, we pave the way for profound self-improvement and healing. This is a necessary step, but it can be challenging because it typically involves facing painful feelings and old wounds. Here's where the benefits of treatment and introspection shine.

Dr. Irvin Yalom, an early proponent of existential psychotherapy, places a premium on introspection as a critical component of treatment. In his book "Love's Executioner," Mitch Yalom writes that "psychotherapy aims at facilitating the development of self-knowledge and self-awareness, and through that, an increased capacity for choice" (Yalom, 2012). We may make better decisions and live more authentic lives by delving deeper into ourselves and learning more about our thought and behavior patterns.

In "The Path of True Healing," the author provides readers with evidence-based methods for healing trauma, as well as strategies for building self-awareness and self-compassion. I base my arguments on my research findings and the studies of eminent psychologists and neuroscientists. Readers will acquire insight into their healing process by discussing themes including emotional regulation, self-compassion, and somatic therapy.

As noted, neuroscientist Dr. Daniel Siegel argues in his book "Mindsight," "when we become aware of our thoughts, feelings, and bodily sensations, we can cultivate greater well-being and resilience" (Siegel, 2010). Finding our way back to our genuine selves and learning to handle life's inevitable trials with more extraordinary grace and ease is the essence of healing.

I intend this book to be a resource for people ready to make positive changes and heal from past hurts. We can all go toward greater emotional freedom and inner serenity by accepting our humanness and making deliberate progress toward self-awareness and self-compassion.

TABLE OF CONTENTS

STEP 1

Identifying what you are healing from

"Although a rose has thorns, its beauty and smell can help mend broken hearts. - I am recovering from the wounds inflicted by toxic relationships and opening myself up to the wonders of the world around me."

Rose's mother married Rose's stepfather when Rose was relatively little. She was relieved that her mother had finally located a reliable caretaker. She had a lot of affection for her stepfather initially, but that changed when he began touching her improperly.

Rose was at a loss for what to do with him at first, so she avoided him. But then, one day, he sexually assaulted her, which was the turning point. Rose's mother didn't trust her when she attempted to tell her. Her stepfather was a deceptive rich man who could provide for the family.

Rose kept silent about the sexual assault for a long time. She finally snapped and attacked her stepfather after he assaulted her again. Rose got away because her mother witnessed the crime and then admitted guilt.

After what happened, Rose felt an overwhelming sense of guilt. She couldn't decide if the abuse hurt more or her mother's unwillingness to confront the reality of it. For a long time, she suffered from clinical depression, anxiety, and post-traumatic stress disorder.

However, Rose eventually decided to get assistance. She finally connected with a therapist who guided her toward healing. Once Rose met a man who truly loved her for who she was, she could trust him again.

Rose's new spouse encouraged her to keep seeing a therapist. In the process of getting better, she realized she didn't have to blame herself for her stepfather's behavior. She finally began to forgive herself and envision a promising future after taking control of her situation.

It is impossible to overstate the importance of recognizing and facing traumas to attain recovery. Rose's tale exemplifies the bravery, resolve, and resiliency of those who refuse to allow their history to determine their future. Unfortunately, Rose's stepfather's violent treatment of her is not an isolated incident. What truly distinguishes her, though, is her insistence on not remaining silent and on actively seeking assistance.

Rose was first unable to comprehend the severity of her situation and hence was compelled to tolerate the assault. In addition, she had her faith in others broken when her mother didn't believe her when she told her about the assault. Rose's mental health suffered due to her prolonged feelings of betrayal and remorse.

Nonetheless, she took charge of her situation and was able to get aid when she finally refused to keep quiet and confronted her stepfather. This led to her meeting with a therapist who assisted her in processing the traumatic experiences she had gone through. Rose was able to begin the complex process of forgiving herself for the abuse with the aid of her therapist and her new partner.

The importance of having loved ones who have your back is emphasized throughout Rose's story. Having someone to talk to, be it a friend, family member, or professional, can help tremendously in the recovery process. It's helpful to have loved ones who will back you up and encourage you on your path to recovery.

Taking responsibility for one's life is another valuable lesson. Rose didn't give in to the temptation to feel sorry for herself. She did not sit back and do nothing but went to her stepfather for assistance. Rose took charge of her life and set herself on the road to recovery by doing this.

The road to recovery may be lengthy, but it is possible and well worth traveling. It's important to be gentle with yourself, acknowledge that healing takes time, and accept that taking things slowly is OK. Anyone who has endured trauma should get professional care immediately. When we recognize our wounds, assume responsibility for our healing, and surround ourselves with positive influences, we can begin to feel better.

Healing is not simply a mental or emotional process but a physical one. We tend to ignore or deny our suffering and trauma, which makes it hard to determine where we stand in terms of healing. We must face our past traumas and decide what we need to heal from to go on and find inner peace.

The first step is realizing we have a broken part of ourselves and accepting help. This could happen to us recently, or we've been repressing our history. Whatever the case may be, we have to admit that we're not doing fine and that we need to make some adjustments if we want to get anywhere.

When we aren't ready to address the source of our pain, it might not be easy to pinpoint where we need healing. Perhaps we are avoiding facing our traumas because we are in denial or because we fear the agony that will inevitably arise. When this happens, it's common to want to avoid dealing with our feelings by focusing on something else or stuffing them down.

Burying our feelings and pretending they aren't there can only worsen matters. If we don't deal with our traumatic experiences, we'll keep feeling its effects, whether or not we realize it. Unresolved trauma can create anxiety, sadness, and other mental health problems.

Therefore, we must persuade ourselves of the necessity of recovery. This could include visiting a therapist or close friend, starting a journal, or practicing yoga or meditation. The first step toward recovery begins with recognizing suffering and the deliberate decision to face it head-on.

Having accepted the fact that we need healing, we must now determine what it is that we wish to mend. To do so, we may need to reflect on our past behaviors and consider how they affected our feelings and responses. This is not always easy, as it may involve thinking about or feeling unpleasant things.

However, the benefits justify the effort. Finding the source of our wounds is the first step toward recovering from them and learning from their lessons. The effects of trauma on our behavior and relationships may become apparent over time. Some of our emotional difficulties and trust issues with others may make more sense. Healing begins with this kind of introspection.

Considerations of recent or historical traumas can help us determine what we need to overcome. Neglect, abuse, the death of a loved one, or a catastrophic incident like a car crash or a natural disaster are all examples of such traumatic experiences. Everyone's experience of trauma is unique and deserves respect, so we should avoid making comparisons.

It's helpful to take stock of our actions and feelings and look for recurring themes. For instance, if we're avoiding certain things in life due to a traumatic experience, it may be time to face up to it and move on. Similarly, if we're having trouble with anxiety or depression, it could be because of a traumatic experience we haven't dealt with.

Further, we might examine how our trauma manifests in our interpersonal connections. If, as adults, we have a hard time accepting our worth, it may be because we were never taught to do so as children. A history of betrayal or isolation may be the root of any problems trusting or connecting with others.

Ultimately, self-reflection and honesty are required to determine the source of our desire for healing. To heal and go on, we must face the anguish and tragedy that has befallen us. It's not easy, but it will be well worth it in the long run. We can make a better future for ourselves and others we care about if we can put the past to rest.

7 Reasons Why Understanding What Hurt Us Help us in Our Pathway to Healing

1. Increased Self-Awareness: When we comprehend and recognize what harms us, we better understand our thoughts, emotions, and actions. This heightened self-awareness lays the groundwork for rehabilitation.

2. Breaking Cycles: Knowing what hurts us is a critical first step toward changing negative cycles and habits that keep us rooted and stuck in the past.

3. Empowerment: Knowing our vulnerabilities can be a potent source of strength. It empowers us to alter our

circumstances for the better. When we know what hurt us and face it, we gain the power to heal.

4. Clarity: Knowing the core of our pain provides us transparency about what we must do to recover. It gives us an apparent path to follow on our recuperation journey.

5. Forgiveness: Knowing what has injured us can open us to forgiveness. It can enable us to understand the motives of those who have hurt us and authorize us to pardon them.

6. Healing the Inner Child: Familiarity with what damages us can assist us in reconnecting with our inner child and healing emotional wounds that may have been held up into adulthood.

7. Freedom: Ultimately, awareness and knowing what hurts us can create a sense of freedom. It permits us to let go of the past, live fully in the present, and look forward to the future.

Activity

HEALING BOARD

Here are the instructions for creating a healing board for you to understand your healing process:

1. Get a large piece of cardboard or poster board, and decorate it with colors and designs that inspire you and promote relaxation and healing.

2. Write a clear and concise statement on the board that defines your healing journey. For example, "I am healing from (condition or illness), and I am confident in my ability to overcome it."

3. List the reasons why you want to heal. This can include personal goals, such as being able to play with your children or return to your job, and emotional motivations, such as wanting to feel more confident and happy.

4. Create a special section on the board that lists your strengths and skills. Remind yourself of everything you are good at and reflect on those skills that can help you overcome any obstacles you may face in your healing journey.

5. Use the board to track your progress, with pictures and updates that show how far you have come. This can inspire a sense of accomplishment and reinforce your dedication to your healing process.

6. Finally, surround yourself with positivity. Use the board as a visual reminder of your progress, determination, and inner strength. This will help you stay focused on your goal and inspire you to keep moving despite setbacks.

Remember, the healing board is a tool to help you stay motivated and focused on your journey. It can be a powerful tool to reinforce your commitment to your path and help you stay centered and focused on your wellness goals.

Write your journal here!

(Write your learning on the First Step Towards Path Of Healing using the space provided with the direction based on the theme given below)

"The Journey Begins: Identifying What You're Healing From"

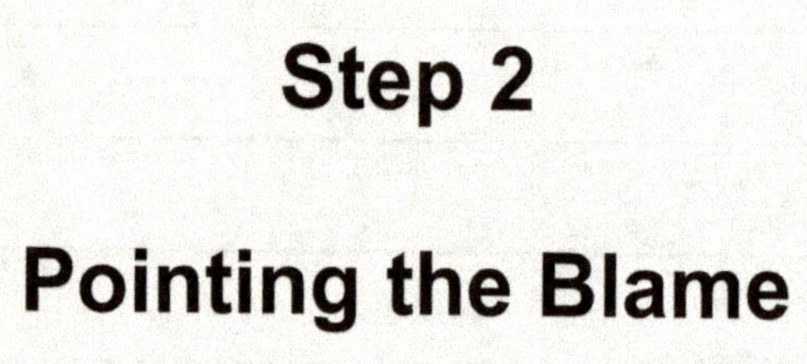

Step 2

Pointing the Blame

"Facing your trauma is like staring down a hungry lion; it's terrifying, overwhelming, and intimidating. But you must confront your trauma head-on if you are ever to overcome it and recover your life, just as the hunter must confront the lion if he is ever to kill it."

Leon had a less-than-ideal upbringing. His family was falling apart, and he saw each of his siblings spiral farther and more into hopelessness. Two of his siblings died from Covid-19, his sister became a prostitute, and his brother sold drugs and went to prison. Their father was a violent drinker, and their mother had abandoned them, adding insult to injury.

Leon found consolation in sports as he navigated a difficult childhood filled with turmoil and poverty. He used his suffering as fuel for his athletic pursuits. The only way out of their precarious predicament, he realized, was for him to get an education.

Leon graduated from high school with honors despite his alcoholic father's threats and abuse. However, that wasn't all he did. He brought the same determination and grit to the classroom that he showed on the field. He and his alcoholic father struggled financially, but he worked hard at a nearby convenience shop to make ends meet.

He was able to graduate from college with Latin honors by channeling all his suffering. He got a decent job because of his perseverance. Leon had defied the odds, and his rough upbringing would not define him. Instead, he decided to take on each obstacle head-on, using them to motivate himself to greater heights.

Leon is now considered a role model by many in his neighborhood. He has not only disproved the notion that his troubled past defines him but also shown that every individual can overcome adversity. His perseverance and commitment to realizing his goals have served as an inspiration to his fellow students. Anyone who has faced hardship might find inspiration in Leon's tale.

Leon's experience illustrates how one may overcome adversity and go on with life. Leon had a difficult life, but he used it to motivate himself closer to his ambitions.

Leon's commitment to furthering his studies significantly contributed to his success. By doing so, he not only improved his employability but also became an expert in his field, inspiring others around him.

One crucial part of Leon's progress was his willingness to face his problems squarely. He didn't allow the alcoholic father or the deaths of his brothers to slow him down. Instead, he was able to use his hardships as driving forces in his life.

Perhaps most importantly, Leon's tale demonstrates that with the right attitude and support, anyone can triumph over hardship. He didn't allow his past to hold him back from a brighter future; instead, he used it as motivation. His dedication and persistence can motivate others to work hard, too.

In the end, Leon's experience demonstrates that despite the difficulty, it is possible to overcome adversity and trauma. Healing and a better future are possible if we can learn to use our hardships as fuel for change, surround ourselves with helpful people and resources, and tackle problems head-on.

Recognizing and dealing with the causes of our suffering is an integral part of the often-protracted process of healing from trauma. This involves laying blame at the feet of people who may have unwittingly or deliberately added to our painful experiences. Confronting these people can be difficult, but it's necessary for healing and moving on.

The first step in dealing with the persons who may have caused our trauma is pinpointing who they are. Any person, whether parent, sibling, friend, romantic partner or stranger, could fit this category. The next step, after figuring out who has to be confronted, is coming up with a strategy for doing so.

One solution is to put our thoughts and feelings into writing and send it to the individual who caused us distress. This strategy can be helpful for people who are uncomfortable with confrontation or want time to think about what they will say before speaking up. However, we should remember that the other person could not react as we expect or might not even notice our suffering, so we should be mentally and emotionally ready for any possibility.

Direct communication, whether in person or over the phone, is another viable alternative. This can be stressful and emotionally draining, but it can also lead to a quicker conclusion and a better understanding of the issue. We should go into the conversation knowing exactly what we want to say and what we hope to accomplish, and we should also be mentally and emotionally ready to handle whatever comes up in the talk.

Alternately, some people find it helpful to talk to a therapist or counselor about their traumatic experiences, to process the hurt and fury that may arise from seeing their abusers. Taking time to process and fortify our emotional fortitude before confronting the other person directly can be a more gradual and supportive strategy.

Some people find it beneficial to find a physical way to release their emotional distress. One option is to visit a "rage room" where destructive behavior is encouraged in a controlled environment. Even if this doesn't solve the problem or get us to talk to the person who caused us harm, it can be an excellent first step in processing our feelings and moving on with our lives.

Finally, it may be necessary to cut the individual out of our lives. This may involve severing ties with a toxic relative or quitting a loving partnership that has proven harmful. It's difficult to cut someone out of your life when they're doing more harm than good, but you must put your mental health and happiness first.

Identifying those we owe accountability for our trauma and having that conversation is crucial to our recovery. There are a variety of approaches one can take, and it's vital that an individual figure out which one works best for them, given their unique set of circumstances and emotional requirements. Facing our trauma head-on is a powerful act of self-care that can lead to more calm and emotional healing in the long run, even though it may be challenging and emotionally intense in the short term.

7 Ways to Confront Trauma towards Path of Healing.

Trauma is an emotional, physical, and psychological response to a deeply distressing or disquieting event. It can be hard to confront and process traumatic events, but finding ways to do so is essential. When the pain of trauma becomes too much to bear, it can be tempting to point blame to find relief. But focusing on accountability does not lead to true healing, and identifying healthy ways to confront trauma is the key to actual resolution.

1. Identify Your Feelings: When faced with trauma, it is essential to be mindful of the emotions resulting. Take time to identify the feelings of anger, hurt, guilt, anxiety, and fear that can arise in response to trauma. Being mindful of these feelings can help you process them healthier.

2. Speak Up: It can be challenging to talk about trauma, but speaking up is essential to begin the healing process. Find a safe space to tell your story and express the emotions that come with it. Talking to trusted family members, friends, or professionals can help to provide a supportive environment for healing.

3. Find Ways to Cope: Allow yourself time to grieve and find healthy ways to cope with the pain of trauma. Take care of your physical and mental health by eating well, exercising, and getting enough sleep. Engage in activities that bring you joy, such as listening to music, writing, or spending time with friends.

4. Reach Out for Support: Talking to friends and family can give you a sense of comfort and understanding. You may also consider seeking professional help from a therapist or counselor. This can help to provide a safe place to explore the traumatic experience and develop healthier ways of dealing with the pain.

5. Let Go of Blame: Pointing blame can be an easy way to avoid the complex emotions associated with trauma. Focusing on accountability does not lead to true healing and can instead cause more hurt and pain. Acknowledge the harrowing events that led to the trauma and find ways to forgive the blame.

6. Practice Self-Compassion: Be kind and understanding to yourself, and extend the same compassion to others. Self-compassion can help reduce guilt and self-blame and cultivate feelings of understanding and acceptance.

7. Make Meaning of the Experience: Trauma can be a source of growth and strength. Reflect on the experience and try to make meaning of it. What have you learned? How can this experience help you to move forward?

Activity

Trauma is a challenging experience to navigate, but there are ways to confront it and heal. Identifying and expressing emotions, finding ways to cope, reaching out for support, and letting go of blame are essential steps to resolving trauma. With time and effort, it is possible to find a path of healing.

1. Find a place where you won't be disturbed, preferably private and quiet.

2. Establish a routine: write in your journal regularly. A sense of stability and ease may result.

3. Incorporate purpose into your journaling by taking a few minutes to reflect on why you keep a diary in the first place, whether it be to process feelings, recognize trends, or inquire about new experiences.

4. Start each time you write in your journal with a grounding activity, such as deep breathing or mindfulness meditation, to help you focus and be in the now.

5. Let your thoughts and feelings flow freely by writing without censorship, regulations, or evaluation.

6. Be honest in your writing; don't hold anything back. Feel free to let out any negative or upsetting emotions you may be experiencing.

7. If you're feeling overwhelmed or triggered, stop what you're doing and take a break. Pay attention to your physical signs and put your mental and emotional health first.

8. Conclude on a positive note: At the close of each diary entry, consider writing an expression of appreciation or an objective for the next day.

Journaling can be an effective method for processing and dealing with traumatic experiences. Here are some suggestions for using journals to deal with difficult situations:

1. List topics you wish to write about in your diary, such as traumatic experiences, fears, or relationship difficulties.

2. Use questions like "How does this issue affect me?" and "What emotions am I feeling about this issue?" as writing prompts to help you focus your journal entries.

3. Look for structures or recurrent ideas in your writing and investigate them. If you keep a journal, you may be able to pinpoint specific events or behaviors that are causing or exacerbating the problem.

4. Examine your journal entries from the past to discover how your feelings and outlook have evolved.

5. Plan: Write your plans for the future and how you hope to solve the problem in your journal.

Take your time and be kind to yourself. Even while journaling can be a helpful habit, if you ever feel like you need more support or aid, it's best to talk to a professional.

Write your Journal!

Write your learning on the second Step, Towards Path Of Healing, using the space provided with the direction based on the theme given below)

"Breaking Free from Blame: Pointing the Finger

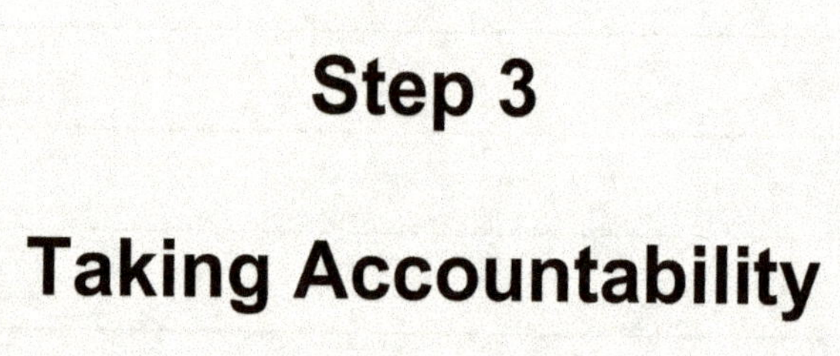

Step 3

Taking Accountability

"Taking responsibility is like a raven; it can be scary at first, but in the end, it will set you free and help you grow,"

Omar was a loyal and diligent Arab who took pride in his background. Omar believed he could make a difference by being an honest and ethical worker at his major organization, despite the company's history of corruption.

However, the corporation eventually said they would let several people go, including Omar. Omar was crushed to find he was being allowed to go from his job despite his stellar performance.

Worse, worse, he quickly learned the real cause for his dismissal. Omar's race played a role in the company's decision to lay him off to save money. He felt misled and extremely saddened by the open discrimination he had experienced.

Omar's confidence in fellow humans waned. Why did friendly people have to suffer? He had no reason to believe that the world was a just place to live.

As Omar struggled to accept his predicament, he recognized he needed to consider what he could have done better to avoid this injustice. Although he had always worked honestly and diligently, he wondered if he had done enough to combat the corruption he witnessed daily.

Omar's sudden insight gave him the resolve to speak out against injustice. He decided to learn more about activism and share his discrimination story with others.

Omar eventually landed a job where he could make an impact without compromising his principles. Even though he was still dealing with the pain of his past, he believed he was progressing toward recovery by working to make the world a better place for everyone.

The narrative of Omar is an inspiring example of the value of personal responsibility and accountability in the face of oppression. Omar was heartbroken after being fired unfairly because of his race. He couldn't fathom why discrimination was unavoidable or good people frequently fell victim to rigged institutions.

Omar could have given in to hopelessness, but instead, he took decisive action. He realized he had to think about what he could have done differently to prevent the wrong from happening to him. He realized his part in the fight against injustice after doing some soul-searching. After reflecting on his past actions, he acknowledged that he could have done more to combat these injustices.

Omar's life changed forever after he realized this. He didn't wallow in his suffering and resentment but sought to help others through his story. He started reading up on activism and spoke about his experience with prejudice to get others involved in the fight against discrimination.

Omar had a newfound sense of fulfillment and significance in his career. The anguish and rage he felt were transformed into motivation for action. While he was still processing the trauma of his past, he found solace in the knowledge that he was helping to heal the world in the process.

What we can learn from Omar's experience is the importance of owning up to our mistakes and making amends for them. It's easy to point fingers when subjected to unfair treatment or discrimination. This mentality, however, serves merely to reinforce feelings of helplessness and victimhood.

Instead, we must ask ourselves how to improve and work from there. It is up to each of us to play a part in making the world a more equitable and just place. This includes calling out wrongdoing, working for reform, and accepting responsibility for one's acts and those of others.

Like the raven in the fable, accepting responsibility can be terrifying at first. However, it can free us, just like the raven. Taking personal accountability gives us strength and control over our lives. Having done all that we can to improve the world, we may move forward with confidence and conviction.

The path to recovery lies in owning up to mistakes, accepting responsibility, and improving. Omar's tale is a poignant reminder that we all have the potential to make the world a better place, even in the face of adversity.

7 Rule For Taking Accountability Towards the Path Of Healing

Accepting responsibility is a cornerstone of success in business and life in general. It's a great way to learn more about yourself and develop emotionally, making it an integral part of recovery. To progress, we must own up to our mistakes and make amends. Here are seven ways in which accepting responsibility can help you heal:

1. Recognize and accept responsibility for your errors. Recognizing and accepting responsibility for your errors is the first step towards adopting accountability. Realize that blunders are inevitable and use them as opportunities to grow.

2. Don't pass the buck or make excuses for your actions; take full ownership of your decisions and the consequences. Though it may be difficult, taking ownership of one's actions is essential for personal growth and success.

3. If required, make amends after admitting wrongdoing and taking responsibility for it. Apologizing, fixing the problem, or compensating the victim are all possible ways to make amends.

4. Mistakes are inevitable, so it's helpful to examine what went wrong and draw lessons from the experience. The only way to gain wisdom and develop emotionally is via the experience of making errors.

5. Increased self-awareness and development might result from accepting complete responsibility for one's activities. Instead of pointing fingers at others, it makes us examine ourselves and the bigger picture.

6. Move on with optimism and look forward to better times ahead rather than ruminating on the past. Taking responsibility for our actions is a fantastic method for developing from our missteps.

7. It's crucial to show the same mercy to oneself as one would to others and forgive past transgressions. As a result, we can put the past behind us and accept greater responsibility for our future actions.

Accepting responsibility can aid our emotional growth and healing by giving us new perspectives. Taking responsibility and making amends can be easier with this guide.

Activity

HEALING ACCOUNTABILITY PLAYING CARDS

The participants will create accountability cards to help them take charge of their recovery processes. Participants will be asked to make healing accountability cards with positive affirmations, goals, and reminders. They can use the cards as daily cues or reminders to keep moving forward in their healing process. The accountability cards can be used in a group context to provide extra support and encouragement, but the activity can also be done independently.

Write your journal!

HEAL

(Write your learning on the 3rd Step Towards Path Of Healing using the space provided with the direction based on the theme given below)

"Accountability as a Key Step towards Healing"

Step 4

Detox from what has hurt You

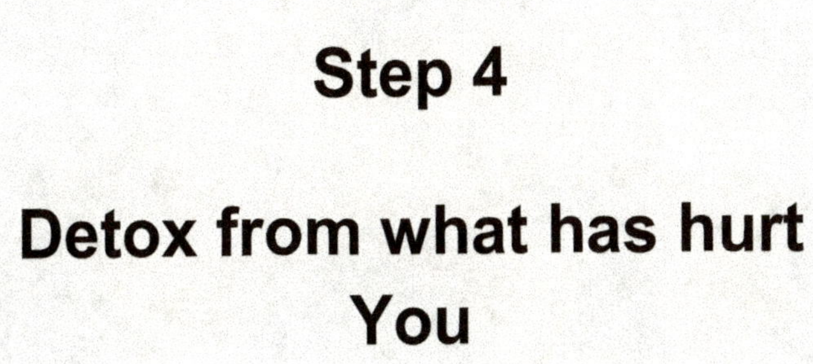

"Like a bee sting to a sunflower, detoxification from hurt and neglect can set off the healing process that ultimately results in a person blossoming into their fullest potential."

There was a young girl once whose name was Sara. She was born into an affluent family and was provided for in every way imaginable, except for the love and care of her parents. They had little time for Sara because of their hectic job and social schedules. Instead, she spent her time with her nanny, whom she loved more than either of her parents.

Sara realized as she got older that her parents weren't giving her enough attention regarding her four primary love languages (quality time, tenderness, acts of service, and physical touch). Despite her financial comforts, she felt unwanted and irrelevant. Sara gradually disliked social interaction and began withdrawing from her family. She struggled to make and maintain close friendships.

One day, though, that all altered. Ovarian cancer was the diagnosis given to Sara. Sara was shocked that nobody she knew at work or in her social circle was concerned about her health. She was lonely and alone, and she needed someone to care for and stand by her.

Sara then recognized that the scars her parents had ignored were beginning to resurface. She knew she needed to mend, but she didn't know how. She decided to cleanse herself of her pain at that point.

Sara started by going through a mental detox and seeing a therapist who assisted her in processing the traumatic experiences she had as a youngster. She also made time to tend to her soul by devoting herself to her faith. She began a regular practice of prayer and meditation in which she communicated with God.

Sara also undertook a physical detox by modifying her food, increasing her exercise, and surrounding herself with encouraging and optimistic individuals. She finally realized the only way forward was to focus on healthy relationships and abandon the poisonous ones.

Sara learned it is worth the time and work it takes to heal. She realized she didn't have to allow the hurtful things that had happened to her in the past to keep hurting her. Through accepting the concept of detoxification, she was able to move on with her life and find the people who would love her for who she was rather than what she had.

Sara's story shows us that letting go of pain and moving on is a challenging journey. To face our suffering and release it requires work, time, and courage. Understanding where our suffering originates and how it has affected our lives is the first step toward recovery.

Seeking the counsel of a trained therapist is the first step toward recovery. Therapy provides a safe space to work through difficult emotions and learn new coping mechanisms. We must also make time for spiritual practices like prayer, meditation, and mindfulness to keep our minds and hearts healthy.

Physical detoxification through adopting a healthy lifestyle is as important as mental detoxification. Changing our eating habits, exercising more, and surrounding ourselves with positive people are all essential parts of this process. Remember that healing is a process that considers your mental, bodily, and spiritual health as a whole.

The last and most crucial step toward recovery is accepting that we can eventually move past the hurt and wounds of the past. We must stop focusing on keeping negative people in our life and start surrounding ourselves with positive, uplifting people.

In the end, we can learn from Sara's experience and realize that it is possible to overcome past hurts. It all starts with admitting we have a problem, getting some assistance, and cutting ties with those who aren't good for us. A revitalized sense of optimism and inner calm can be ours via self-care, healthy relationships, and a positive outlook.

7 Simple Steps To Detoxify from Hurts and Pain that Lingers in Us

Long-term effects on our physical, emotional, mental, social, and spiritual health from neglect, injuries, and abuse can make the road to healing and recovery appear insurmountable. Detoxification methods, however, can aid in the healing process and provide hope for a future that is healthier, more secure, and more in control.

1. Detoxify your body by tending to your physical well-being. Restoring hormonal and systemic equilibrium can be accomplished by eating a diet high in fruits, vegetables, whole grains, and lean meats while reducing sugar, salt, and harmful fats. Stress can be diminished, and strength and stamina can be improved by regular exercise.

2. Detoxifying the mind and spirit from the poison of neglect, injuries, and abuse can be accomplished in several ways. The ability to detect the symptoms of trauma and understand what sets off such reactions is crucial. Seeking out a therapist or joining a support group can be beneficial. It's vital that people feel safe enough to express their feelings.

3. When you detox your mind, you free it from anxious and unpleasant thoughts. Mindfulness meditation, yoga, and similar practices can be beneficial here. Visualization and re-framing destructive thought patterns are only two examples of positive thinking practices that can be useful in

this context. A busy and overactive mind might benefit significantly from some downtime spent doing nothing but resting and relaxing.

4. Detoxing from our social lives is crucial to our recovery. We were finding and spending time with individuals who are accepting, compassionate, and accepting of where you are vital. Comfort and happiness can also be gained through engaging in activities that encourage self-care.

5. Spiritual Detox: Forgiveness and prayer are potent spiritual instruments for overcoming the effects of abuse, neglect, and the like in one's history. It can be very freeing to pray for the strength to let go of bitterness and forgive people who have wronged you. Negative feelings caused by trauma can be mitigated by surrounding yourself with positive affirmations and encouraging words.

6. Detoxing one's environment is an essential part of cleansing one's body and mind. Avoid negative energy or distractions at home or in the office. The ability to think and act constructively is aided by an environment that is safe, quiet, and tranquil.

7. Remember the importance of self-care and self-love. The healing process can be aided by relaxation and doing things that provide joy. Taking time for self-care and self-love can reveal sources of distress, facilitate their release, and spark onward momentum.

When applied in tandem, these seven methods can facilitate physical, emotional, mental, social, and spiritual recovery from the effects of prior neglect, injuries, and abuse. The path to a happier, healthier, and more secure existence is not always easy to find, but it may be paved with hard work and perseverance.

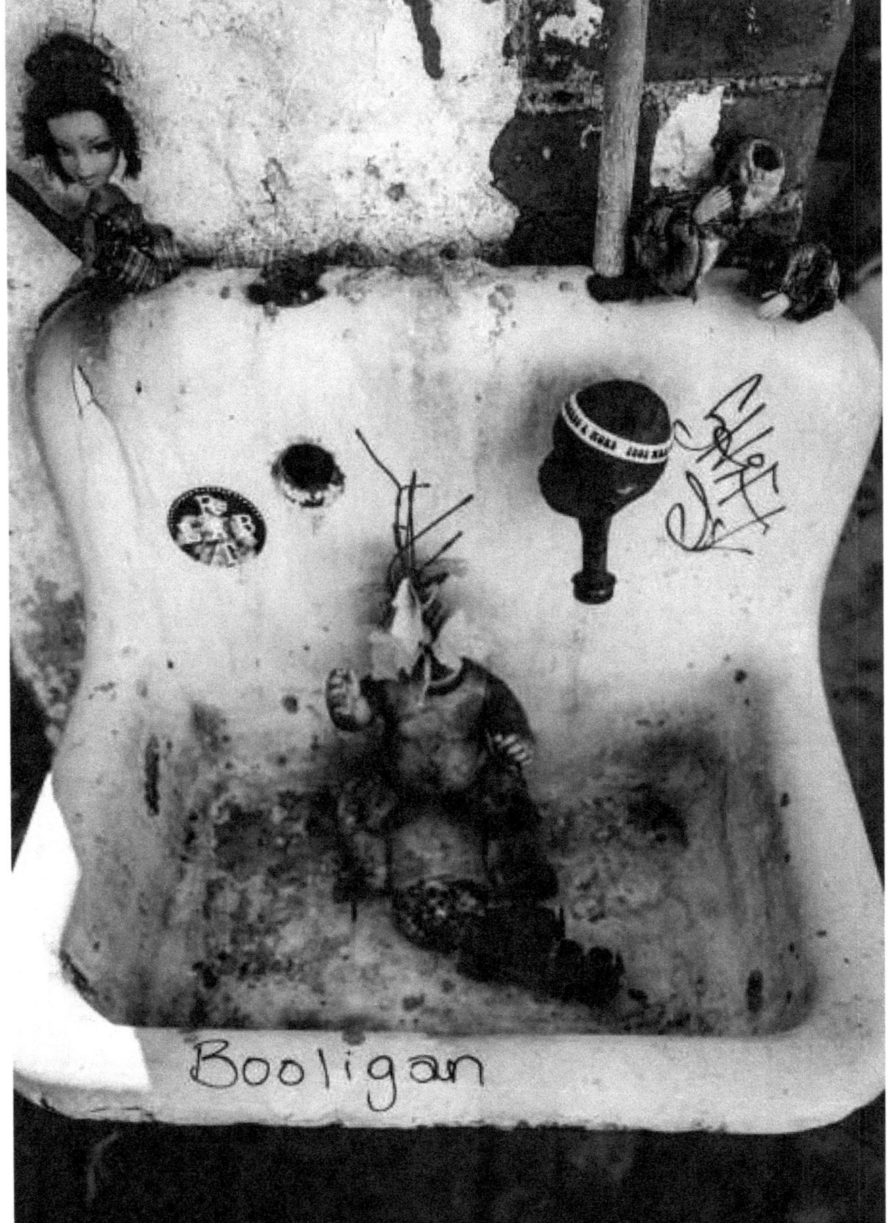

Booligan

Activity

STICKER NOTES FOR MOVING ON

The purpose of this activity is to encourage participants to purge themselves of the toxic effects of unwanted experiences by committing them to paper. (group or alone)

Materials:
Sticky notes, plus marker pens, are required materials.

1. Gather everyone together and get the materials ready to hand out.

2. Have them reflect on painful experiences they'd like to put behind them.

3. Have them use a marker pen to record each occurrence on a sticky note.

4. Tell them to make as many notes as needed.

5. Ask them to write down everything that happened and then post it on a wall or board.

6. Have them read the notes and allow themselves to feel whatever emotions arise without wallowing in them.

7. Then, number each note and have them remove it before crumpling or discarding it.

8. Having the participants feel lighter and more at ease as they let go of each experience is step number eight.

9. Remind them that it may take some time to detox from adverse events in their lives fully and that letting go is a process.

Finally, healing and progress require letting go of past hurts and disappointments. Sticker notes can make it easier to record and disseminate this information. Instruct the group to keep utilizing the technique as long as it takes to rid themselves of useless things.

Write Your Journal!

(Write your learning on the 4th Step Towards Path Of Healing using the space provided with the direction based on the theme given below)

"Detoxing from the Pain: Steps to Let Go and Move Forward"

Step 5

Identifying Triggers you didn't know were there.

"Triggers can be a double-edged sword, reminding us of our pain but also revealing our strength."

Percy had a reputation as a "mama's boy" from an early age. He had a close relationship with his mother and routinely sought her advice on matters of minor importance. But that was a major roadblock in his pursuit of a steady girlfriend. Several failed relationships led him to conclude that he judged women according to his mother's standards.

One of his relationships lasted for three years. His mother could not develop an emotional bond with his girlfriend, even though he was pretty content with her. She insisted her son end things with his girlfriend, and he complied. Percy's feelings for the girl he loved were severely wounded, but he understood he had to emerge from under his mother's shadow.

He looked into his background to find the causes he had overlooked. After his father abandoned her and left him to care for her, he saw her as a manipulative and hurt lady. The lesson he took away was that if someone has hurt you, it's best to figure out why they injured you so you can avoid making the same mistakes in the future.

Percy grew from his experiences and began to believe in himself. He realized he could choose himself without constantly seeking his mother's approval. He realized that his mother's expectations for him were not necessarily his own.

Percy realized that one of the first steps toward making positive changes in one's life is to become aware of the factors that serve as triggers. Identifying the origins of one's own beliefs and practices is crucial. By digging into your history, you can pinpoint the exact moments when you react out of hurt from your past. From there, you may take steps toward making your life your own and living it how you want.

The events in Percy's life demonstrate how a prior trauma was interfering with his present-day relationships and preventing him from settling down with a woman. Despite appearances, he unfairly judged women by his mother's standards because of their tight relationship.

Triggers are the things that set off reactions in us, usually without our even realizing it at the time. Our prior experiences can serve as powerful catalysts that shape our present and future. For Percy, it was his upbringing at the hands of his mother that set the tone for how he views and treats women.

To grow and heal as individuals, we must first be able to recognize these triggers and then take action to eliminate them. Understanding where our ideas and activities come from is the first step in altering them for the better. Although challenging, this process is essential for our development and happiness since it forces us to confront and evolve from our demons.

Following Percy's path to recovery and self-awareness is an excellent reminder of the value of recognizing and overcoming personal triggers. Then, and only then, can we shatter chains of self-defeating thought and action and experience true freedom.

7 Ways to Understand Healing of Memory and Avoiding Triggers

Mental health is an essential part of overall well-being, and memories can be one of the most potent triggers for unhealthy emotions. Triggers from memories can lead to negative thoughts and behavior. While we cannot erase or forget our memories entirely, several steps exist to cope with the triggers and heal the memory.

1. Recognize the Memory: Recognizing is the first step to overcoming triggers from memories. Ofreness of the source of the motivation can help us address the emotion it brings. By understanding the associated feelings, we can work to manage them more effectively.

2. Acknowledge the Emotion: We should not ignore or suppress the emotions associated with the memory. Even if it is painful, deserving it and allowing ourselves to experience it can benefit from it.
3. Practice Self-Compassion: Self-compassion can help us harbor strong support system. Instead of thinking of our triggers and memories as something to be ashamed of, we should accept them with kindness and understanding.

4. Forgiveness: Forgiveness is not about the other person— It is about ourselves. Forgiving ourselves for our mistakes or the heartaches, we experienced can pave the way for mental healing.

5. Talk to Someone: Talking to a friend, a loved one, or a professional counselor can be beneficial in understanding and overcoming the triggers from the memories. They can offer a new perspective to the memories and help us to reframe them healthily

6. Create Positive Memories: It can be helpful to create new memories that are associated with positive emotions. This can effectively overcome the triggers and transform the memory into something more cheerful and reassuring.

7. Find Meaning in the Memory: In some cases, we might be able to find a new meaning to the memory or rethink it as a lesson learned. By finding a positive aspect in it, we can use the memory to shape us into a better version of ourselves.

Triggers from memories can be challenging. However, with the right approach and attitude, we can overcome them and heal from the memory.

Activity

AN EXPRESSION OF "UNPACKING THE PAIN"

The goal is to consider the potential origins of distress and traumas that need mending, to identify their triggers and causes, and to recast these into a message of hope.

Materials:
Colorful pens, colorful paper, and scissors are required.

Instructions:

One-on-One Time:

First, make a list, color-coded by type of experience, of all the traumatic things that have happened to you.

Second, create physical artifacts from paper or cardboard in the form of forms, symbols, or images that symbolize the triggering events or memories that are causing you distress. If you've ever been through a heartbreaking breakup, for instance, you could want to carve the outline of a broken heart.

Third, on a separate piece of paper, jot down the possible causes and triggers of those traumatic experiences. If, for instance, you've had panic attacks, you can benefit from keeping track of the stressful situations and events that came just before them.

Fourth, on a separate paper, consider what lesson of optimism or resilience you may take away from the problematic experiences or traumas. If you survived depression, for instance, you might want to record the lessons you learned about yourself and the value of obtaining treatment.

Fifth, use a cutting tool to create the shapes, symbols, or images that best symbolize your message of optimism. If you want to express optimism, you could, for instance, create a silhouette of a rising sun.

 Sixth, Use colorful pens to jot down your encouragement on the various paper cutouts.

Seventh, on a final sheet of colored paper, glue down all the cutout forms to show the progression from hurt to wholeness. Think about how you came to this point and how your terrible experiences and traumas have changed you.

Group Exercise 2:

First, form couples or small teams out of the whole group.

Second, have everyone in the group use different colored pens to record a variety of traumatic situations they've had.

Third, members of the team or pair discuss the specific events or cues that bring up or remind them of the traumatic experiences they've had.

Fourth, consider the origins of the traumatic events and the lessons they've taught.

Fifth, group members consider the positive lessons they've learned from adversity.

Sixth, Members use colored pens to draw a form or symbol that communicates the message of hope or resilience they wish to share.

Seventh, the group puts together the shapes they cut out on a single piece of colored paper to show the progression from suffering to recovery. Think about how you came to this point and how your terrible experiences and traumas have changed you.

Eight, you'll have each group quickly explain their finished product and its meaning. Require attentive, sympathetic listening as others relate their experiences.

Write your journal!

(Write your learning on the 5th Step Towards Path Of Healing using the space provided with the direction based on the theme given below)

"Uncovering Triggers: Discovering Hidden Emotional Wounds"

Step 6

Putting Me First.

"When our love for God is our foremost priority, unconditional and unselfish, it spills over into our love for ourselves and others. If we don't take the time to love ourselves before we give that love to our friends and family, we'll be unable to provide that love to anyone else. Neglecting the need to love ourselves before our household and others is like breaking our heart - for how can we provide love to your family if there is none within us to give?"

Victoria and David tried for years to start a family but were thwarted by infertility. Victoria could not create a healthy egg because David's sperm count was too low. Nothing they attempted, including numerous therapy, seemed to have any effect.

Victoria was a top executive in Boston, but she focused on starting a family instead of continuing her career. As the family earner, this was a big adjustment for her. Financial difficulties strained their relationship, but they refused to give up on their hope of starting a family.

After a long struggle, Victoria was finally able to conceive. However, while they were getting ready for the birth of their child, they fought over money. David's employment was only adequate, but Victoria's had been quite lucrative until she left work to have a kid. David was upset and irritated by her accusation that he was to blame for the couple's financial woes.

When Victoria unexpectedly miscarried, David felt responsible and hated himself. They could not work through their grief over the child's death and the stresses of poverty as a couple. The separation was very close to happening.

Victoria and David were going through a rough stretch, but a trusted friend reunited them. They had come to value each other's company more than anything else, and neither was willing to risk losing it. After two years of fighting, they made up, and Victoria became pregnant with twins.

Victoria was content to stay home and raise the couple's children while David built a successful business. Victoria's miscarriage crushed her heart, but they could find peace again. They persevered through adversity and came to place their children and their relationship above all else.

They had a difficult path filled with infertility, financial strain, and possible divorce, but they prioritized themselves. They realized the importance of prioritizing their relationships, communication, and love and became better partners and parents to their children than their parents were to them.

The lesson of Victoria and David's story is that we must prioritize and love ourselves first to recover from adversity. Victoria and David persisted in trying to start a family despite infertility and financial challenges. However, while chasing this ideal, they neglected their needs and wants.

Everyone has different hopes and dreams for their future, and they must take the time to discover those desires. To live a happy and fulfilled life, we must take time alone to think about who we want to be and what we want out of life. Victoria put her career on hold to start a family, but the experience taught her the value of striking a healthy balance between the two.

The story also stresses the importance of discussing things and setting relationship priorities. It's crucial to talk to those we care about and find solutions to our difficulties together when we're going through tough times. Victoria and David almost got a divorce when they hit a hard patch, but with the support of a close friend, they were able to work things out and put their family first.

Self-acceptance and self-love are also stressed throughout the narrative. David blamed himself and had a deep sense of self-loathing after Victoria's miscarriage. It's tempting to hold ourselves responsible for our problems, but self-love and compassion are essential even in the most trying times.

The lesson from Victoria and David's story is that we must prioritize ourselves in all aspects of our lives, including our relationships. Healing from trauma and overcoming adversity can be achieved by setting and sticking to realistic goals, maintaining healthy relationships, and treating oneself with kindness and compassion. Never forget the person you worked so hard to become since that's what makes you genuinely exceptional.

7 Essential Tips for Healing by Putting Yourself First

To maintain your health and happiness, you must prioritize yourself occasionally. The better we know ourselves and accept who we are, the more we may enjoy life. Self-care goes beyond simple indulgence. It involves deliberate efforts to maintain a healthy state of being on all levels (physical, mental, and spiritual). Self-care is not egotistical; instead, it is fundamental to our development. Here are seven methods to begin the process of mending and prioritizing yourself:

1. Find Your Passion and Purpose
Discovering your life's calling is a crucial first step to recovery and self-advocacy. Peace of mind and a steady emotional state can be attained through pursuing happiness

and meaning in life. Figure out what drives you and holds you back on your path to success.

2. Understanding oneself

Accurate self-awareness is an in-depth comprehension of one's nature, emotions, and goals. Learn more about who you are and how you interact with the environment by taking note of your routines, recurring thoughts, and routine actions. Mindfulness and receptivity to bodily cues can help us strike a healthy mental-physical balance.

3. Put Limits

Self-care is facilitated by setting appropriate limits for yourself. Define your boundaries and tell others what you will and will not accept from them. Doing so promotes harmony and prosperity in your interpersonal relationships. This can make it easier to have deep conversations without feeling rushed or overwhelmed.

4. Explore the Outdoors

Time spent in natural settings has been associated with positive outcomes, including increased productivity and decreased anxiety. The outdoors allows us to reconnect with nature and, by extension, with ourselves. As a bonus, it makes us more mindful and conscious and reduces obsessive thinking.

5. Exercising

Stress, emotions, and mental health can all benefit greatly from regular physical activity. It causes the body to produce endorphins, which improve our mood and help us unwind.

It's a great way to cultivate awareness and an optimistic attitude.

6. Compassion for oneself
Self-care and insight into the effects of trying times are cornerstones of recovery. Being kind and forgiving, speaking positively to oneself, and practicing mindfulness are all components of self-compassion.

7. Make Friends
Having relationships with other people that are genuine and important to us is crucial to our health. It's critical to have close relationships with upbeat, encouraging people. Indulging in the company of those who genuinely value and respect us can do wonders for our sense of well-being.

Healing and prioritizing oneself should be seen as an individual process with no absolute right or wrong destination. Use your imagination to find new ways to take care of yourself. Never lose sight of caring for your physical, mental, and emotional health as you move through life.

Activity

JAR OF HEARTS

Empowering Self-Love" is a self-guided exercise in overcoming trauma resulting from abuse and other forms of neglect.

The purpose is to participate in a therapeutic activity of introspective nature that fosters a love for oneself and points one along the road to recovery from trauma, hurt, and guilt.

Paper and a jar are the two necessary items.

Instructions:

The first thing you should do is take a deep breath and relax your mind. Take a seat, ideally somewhere quiet, and permit yourself to unwind.

Second, record all the critical thoughts and false beliefs you've held about yourself because of your abuse, hurt, or guilt. Don't hold back or censor your thoughts; jot down all that comes to mind.

The third step is to tuck the paper inside the jar after folding it. Make sure the lid is on tight.

Fourth, jot down all the encouraging words to help you love and care for yourself with compassion and kindness. Phrases like "I am enough," "I am worthy," and "I deserve love and respect" are all examples.

The fifth step is to fold up the affirmations and store them in the jar alongside the negative ones. Blend them.

Sixth, put it to paper and promise to put self-love and good self-talk first, no matter what you've been through. Fold it in half, add it to the top of the jar, and sign it.

Seventh, concentrate by closing your eyes while holding the jar. Recognize the feelings you're experiencing. Then, while tending to your positive affirmations, gradually release your unfavorable ideas.

Eighth, once you've filled your jar, put it somewhere you'll see it often and can get it quickly. Pick one affirmation randomly and repeat it to yourself whenever you feel depressed or when negative ideas enter your mind.

Finally, you will be able to distinguish between the negative self-talk you engage in and the great attributes you already possess, thanks to this exercise. In addition, it fosters the process of overcoming trauma, past hurts, and guilt by making self-love a priority.

Write your journal!

(Write your learning on the 6th Step Towards the Path Of Healing using the space provided with the direction based on the theme given below)

"Putting Yourself First: A Vital Step in the Healing Process"

Steps 7

Elevating in Life (Wanting More)

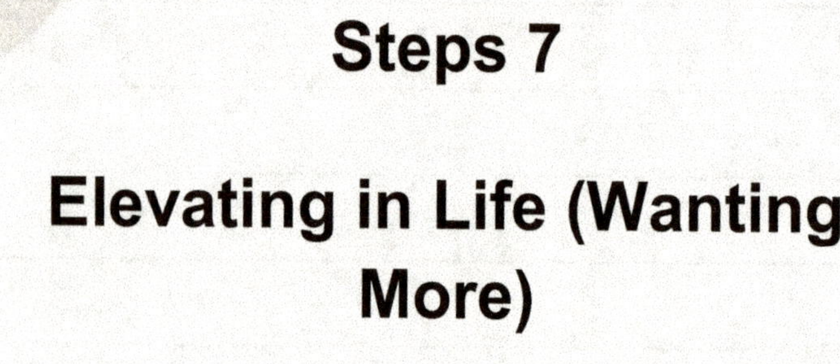

"The weight of abandonment and mistreatment must be released. Put effort into developing yourself, find places to learn, and serve others. Just like a tree, you should be able to withstand adversity and eventually bear fruit."

Growing up was difficult for Julia. Due to their inconsistent open connection, her parents were rarely there for her when she needed them. Her mental health suffered from being abandoned for the most part. She vowed to herself as an adult that she would never make the same mistakes she saw her parents make.

Julia found a husband who encouraged her and let her follow her dream of becoming a public speaker and an inspiration to others. Though she found professional success as a motivational coach and speaker, her family always came first. She hoped her teenage son and young daughter would never experience the same abandonment she had as a child.

Julia realized the need to turn negative emotions into constructive actions. Even though she was extremely busy with work, she made time for her children. She never missed one of their performances or other school-related activities.

Julia's dedication to her work, studies, and passions was never at the expense of her loved ones. She made specific changes to be a happy mom and lead a fulfilling life. She settled on a happy medium. She loved being the parent she was since her childhood mistreatment helped mold her into that person.

The story's moral either allows our past to hold us back or uses it to propel us forward. We can choose to make something good out of our suffering. Julia's story is an inspiration because it shows how far one person can come from a disadvantaged background. We need only focus on good deeds and cultivate loving bonds within our families.

If you feel ignored or abandoned by your parents, growing up can be very difficult. Julia had to fight with her mental health and felt alone because she and her parents didn't communicate openly with each other regularly. But she decided that she wouldn't let her past stop her now. She turned that into motivation to improve herself as a parent and a person.

The events in Julia's life demonstrate the need to channel destructive feelings into positive activity. She concluded that the best way to overcome her pain was to devote herself to constructive endeavors. Despite her hectic schedule, she always found time to attend her kids' school events.

Ultimately, everyone feeling down can find hope in Julia's narrative. It's proof that anything is possible if you put your mind to it, put in the work, and keep a positive outlook. She overcame the challenges she had as a child and is now a robust and confident adult.

Every person has options in this world. Our history can either be a shackle that prevents us from moving forward or a springboard that helps us reach our goals. For her part, Julia went with Option 2. She channeled the strength she gained from her wounds and injuries. She proved that bad experiences might lead to positive growth.

Finally, rerouting our pain isn't always simple, but it's always doable. The lessons from Julia's experience are that the journey's end will be well worth the effort. All we have to do is think positively, strengthen our relationships at home, and draw strength from our experiences to become our best selves.

7 Path Toward Healing and Recovery By Restoring Life

There's a lot of noise in our heads, and it's not always easy to tune it out and concentrate on improving. It might be challenging to go on and direct positive energy when we have witnessed or experienced unpleasant hurt, guilt, resentment, or other trauma. To get back to the way of life, we once had, we need first to acknowledge what has changed, then investigate why, and last, take action to fix the problems we've discovered. We can start the road to recovery and health with various resources and disposal.

First and foremost, you should give yourself time to think and distance yourself emotionally from the painful experience. Consider your hurt and guilt, and pay attention to any associated ideas. Think critically about the situation and ask yourself questions like "What is the harm?" "What is the lesson I must learn?" and "What is the best course of action for me to take now?" By doing so, you can start the healing process with fewer lingering unpleasant feelings.

Second, recognize that suffering is inevitable, and develop the habit of using meditation and positive self-talk to overcome feelings of anger, guilt, and resentment. When we realize that suffering is a natural part of living, we can turn our anguish into wisdom. Start engaging in mindful self-talk that challenges the harmful thoughts and calls the situation by its correct name instead of giving in to the pain and brooding on negative ones.

Third, focus on your response rather than reaction. Response is an act of maturity based on logical approach rather than reaction which dwells on emotions and feelings.

Fourth, stop dwelling on the past and start actively seeking answers to the present issues you're facing. Though we can't alter what has already happened, we may work to better our current situation. It is possible to leave the past behind us and go forward with our lives if we stop to assess the issue and consider our options.

Fifth, try to keep a sunny disposition. We may all begin by realizing that encouraging ourselves to think differently is a powerful tool. Please take responsibility for our negative internal dialogue and work to replace it with more constructive, upbeat thoughts.

Sixth, get back in touch with an old interest or passion. It's crucial to prioritize rest and rejuvenation as we work to overcome the mental and emotional challenges we've faced. Participate in pursuits that bring about joy and contentment.

Finally, consult an expert. If we want to mend the scars of the past, consulting a professional is a terrific idea. A counselor or therapist can provide a secure, judgment-free environment to process feelings of loss and trauma.

In conclusion, try to think positively and create success. Put the knowledge you've gained about healing and recovery to use by focusing on the good things in your life and working hard to make your path to success.

It is possible to heal and restore one's life after suffering from distress, pain, guilt and resentment considers the abovementioned avenues toward healing and restoration. We may regain control of our lives and begin the road to recovery through introspection, expert assistance, problem-solving, optimism, and a concentration on our achievements.

AUTHORIZED
VISITORS ONLY ON
THIRD FLOOR

Activity

POSTER OF RECOVERY

1. Block off some time to dedicate to making your poster. Get your hands on some poster board, some markers, some stickers, and any other embellishments you can think of.

2. Write the poster's title in prominent, bold characters at the top. (Raise the Bar: Turning Adversity into Opportunity for Growth)

3. Locate the middle of the poster board and draw a circle. This ring represents your entire existence.

4. Using the marker, split the circle into quarters. One segment for each area of your life that you want to enhance. You could pick from areas like work, love, health, and development.

5. Write individual objectives in each of the circle's quadrants. Be optimistic and practical while stating your objectives. You can set more realistic goals, such as "I will exercise for 30 minutes a day" instead of "I will lose 20 pounds in a week."

6. In the outer ring, jot down any unfavorable feelings or thoughts you have about your life. A few examples might be "I'm not good enough" and "I always fail."

7. Review the written record of your unpleasant feelings and thoughts. Recognize them, but also question whether or not they hold water. Transform them into upbeat or agnostic language.

8. Put Stickers, photographs, and other decorations that speak to your personality, and the improvements you hope to accomplish in your life should be added at the end.

9. Put your poster where you'll see it frequently. Make it a reminder of your aspirations and how you will turn hurt into strength.

Write your journal!

(Write your learning on the 7th Step Towards the Path Of Healing using the space provided with the direction based on the theme given below)

Elevating Your Life: Pursuing Your Goals and Dreams"

Step 8

Letting Go

"Recovery from trauma and hurtful experiences flows like a river. It may take some time for the river to begin flowing freely again, but with time and patient coaching, the debris will be washed away, and a new route toward completeness will be created."

As a result of his experiences, Charles found it challenging to flourish. He was born into a family of addicts. Thus, he experienced instability and uncertainty at home. His parents were drug addicts who spent most of the day yelling at each other and lashing out at him. Charles's upbringing has never been consistent or warm. As he aged, he increasingly identified with addicts. He was frustrated, discouraged, and sad, with no optimism for the future.

Charles had finally hit rock bottom one day. For weeks, he had considered ending his life because of his distress. In the evening, he had resolved to top it all, and he received a phone call. An old classmate had reached out to him with an invitation to sing in the church choir. Since Charles had never shown any interest in religion before receiving this invitation, he was taken aback. Nonetheless, he felt forced to answer affirmatively.

Something changed as Charles sang that night next to his pal. Now, finally, he felt at home in the world. He felt a fantastic outpouring of support and affection. One of the most fundamental human needs, interpersonal connection, was something he had been lacking. Charles experienced a sense of grace that night.

Charles eventually became an involved churchgoer throughout the subsequent years. He discovered the meaning of mercy, kindness, and love. He began to shift his perspective and recognize that there was more to life than his previous focus on hurt and resentment. However, it was not a smooth ride. Charles's hatred and bitterness towards his parents persisted even though they never managed to sober up. Their addiction ultimately led to their deaths, and he was left to deal with the aftermath.

Charles felt terrible, but he realized he had to forgive his parents to move on with his life. He did not want to carry on his family's tradition of substance abuse. Through therapy and introspection, he discovered the liberating power of letting go. It wasn't simple, but he kept at it. He realized he was doing himself more harm than good by harboring resentment toward his parents. He realized he needed to look past their flaws to appreciate their shared good times.

His parents were only the first people he had to learn to let go of. Charles understood that he had been suppressing a wide range of emotions. He overcame the traumatic experiences of his youth, his struggles with addiction, and his near-death experience through counseling. He eventually found healthy ways to express his feelings and release the burdensome negative ones.

Charles learned the value of surrendering his will to God through these trials. He realized that he was loved and cared for by a higher power and deserved to be happy and in love. He started helping with the church's homeless ministry and other outreach activities. He had never considered that he might find happiness by assisting others, but he did.

Charles has changed so much over the years that he hardly recognizes himself. He has moved past his bitterness and resentment. He has now come to accept and love himself completely. He inspires everyone around him and has helped them overcome their hardships and grief. He has learned from his mistakes and appreciates every day he is given to live.

Charles's life is a powerful illustration of the effects of acceptance, forgiveness, and trust. It's a reminder that things can continuously improve, no matter how bad. Although it may be difficult, letting go is a necessary component of recovery. There will always be obstacles, but Charles is sure of his ability to overcome them. His trust in God, his friends, and the liberating effect of letting remain constant sources of strength for him.

Charles had a troubled upbringing. His life was hell because of his drug addict and violent mom. Charles's upbringing in an antagonistic home imbued him with bitterness, hatred, and rage. Nonetheless, Charles overcame his adversities and developed into a thriving adult. How he accomplished this by letting go of resentment and forgiving his parents for their flaws.

Charles considers learning to let go of one of his life's most valuable lessons. It helped him put the past behind him and look ahead to a brighter future. Keeping grudges and resentment at bay does nothing but feed our dark side and weigh us down. Charles found that admitting his hurt was essential to moving past it. He stopped denying his feelings and embraced the grief and pain he had avoided for so long.

Charles also had to relinquish his resentment and forgive his mother and father. Although it may be difficult, forgiving someone is essential to moving on with your life. Keeping a grudge does nothing but produce mental and emotional instability and distress. When Charles finally released his resentment toward his parents, he could continue his life. It's vital to remember that forgiving those who have injured us is more for our mental health than for the well-being of the one who hurt us.

Charles's path to self-improvement was not a smooth one. He had to accomplish many complicated things, like freeing his family from the grip of evil and falsehood. The effects of his parents' drug abuse were felt deeply by Charles and his siblings. But he knew he couldn't let his parents' choices determine his future. Charles was resolved to end his substance abuse and start a new, sober life.

Charles's optimism about the future was a crucial part of his life-changing experience. He accepted that he could not alter the events of his past, but he could shape his future. This spurred his drive to succeed and leave his troubled upbringing behind him. He zeroed in on what he wanted and did what he needed to do to get it. Because of this, he was able to stop letting his history determine his future and start making his own choices.

Charles's story is motivational for everybody who has ever had to overcome adversity. He shows us that we may triumph over our failures by releasing them, forgiving those responsible, and looking ahead. It's not always simple to let go, yet doing so is essential to our development and recovery. It may hurt at first, but it's necessary if we want to be free of our past. By doing what Charles did and letting go of the past, forgiving, and looking forward, we can create our route to a better future.

7 Processes Of Letting Go
Towards the Path of Healing

Life is full of trauma and getting-that doesn't mean it has to define or rule the remainder of our existence. Letting go is a potent method of overcoming pain and moving on with life. Some preparation is necessary for a successful letting-go experience.

First is recognizing the feelings you're having as a result of the trauma is the first step toward healing. Recognizing our true emotions without judgment or anticipation is crucial. This understanding facilitates a link to our genuine emotions and the processing of the events at hand. The first step toward recovery is gaining insight into our feelings.

The second stage is to acknowledge the suffering and let go of it. We can do this by giving ourselves time and space to accept what has happened, by sobbing, by writing,

134

or by talking about our trauma or pain. Professional assistance in this area, such as that provided by therapists, may be necessary at this stage.

The third action is to create fresh means of dealing with stress. After we've given ourselves time to grieve, we may utilize these tools to help us find healthier methods of coping with the challenges we've faced. Mindfulness training, having a heart-to-heart with a trusted friend or family member, or engaging in a relaxing activity like yoga or music are all examples.

The fourth stage entails doing something about the problem. Although we cannot change the past, we can work to make our lives better and lessen the likelihood that we will again experience such a traumatic occurrence. Possible solutions include having a conversation with the offender, seeking outside assistance, or avoiding a repeat performance.

Reminding ourselves that we have power is the fifth stage. No matter how difficult things get, we always have control over how we react. We have the power to choose whether to look on the bright side or the dark, and whether or not to forgive. This is a tough move, but the outcome is ultimately in our hands.

The sixth stage is to let go and forgive. Realizing that we can't get better while harboring resentment toward someone is crucial. To let go and forward in life, forgiveness is often required, but it is rarely simple.

Acceptance is the seventh and last step. What has happened cannot be undone, but we can learn from it and grow stronger because of it. This is a challenging but essential part of becoming better. Understanding and coming to terms with past events may be very therapeutic and liberating.

Getting past trauma and pain is a challenging but essential path. By patiently working through each of these, we can overcome our pain and find a path to wholeness and healing. It is our responsibility to put in the effort necessary to recover and go on.

Activity

GRATITUDE CALENDAR

Week 1: Reflect and Release

- ❖ Choice a day to recollect on past painful experiences
- ❖ Jot down your feelings and ideas in a journal
- ❖ After contemplating, set a moment to release those negative feelings and thoughts
- ❖ Consider burning the pages or ripping them up and throwing them away

Week 2: Forgiveness Exercise

- ❖ Select a day to forgive someone who has hurt you in the past
- ❖ Write a letter to that person expressing your forgiveness
- ❖ Even if you don't send the letter, it can still be powerful to get your thoughts and feelings down on paper

Week 3: Self-Care Day

- ❖ Schedule a day to focus on yourself and practice self-care
- ❖ Choose activities that make you feel good, such as taking a relaxing bath, going for a walk, or enjoying your favorite hobby
- ❖ Remember that taking care of yourself is crucial in your healing journey

Week 4: Gratitude Practice

- ❖ Pick a day to practice gratitude and focus on the positive aspects of your life
- ❖ Write down at least five things you're thankful for, no matter how small they may seem

- ❖ Purposefully shift your attention away from negativity and toward gratitude

By consistently incorporating these activities into your calendar, letting go of the pain and abuse from the past can become a regular part of your healing journey.

Write your journal!

Of Healing using the space provided with the direction based on the theme given below)

Elevating Your Life: Pursuing Your Goals and Dreams"

Step 9

Reintroducing Myself

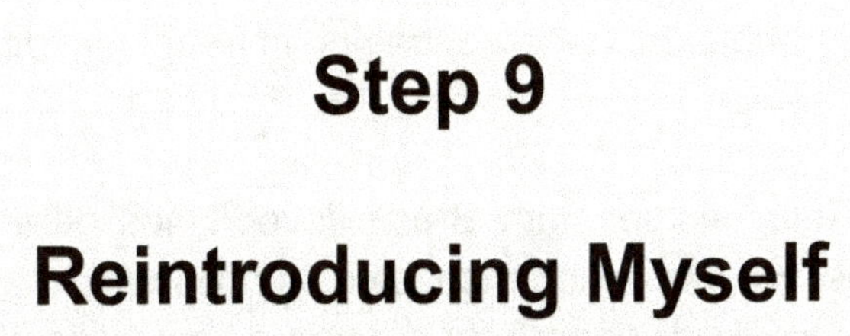

"You can always pick up the pieces and start over with healing, no matter how many times you may have dropped it. Just like an old coin, it can be renewed and reintroduced. Though strange at first, it will quickly prove to be an invaluable resource that you won't want to lose."

Brad once had it all. He was supported by caring loved ones and enjoyed the material comforts provided by his upscale home and steady income. But he developed a gambling addiction, and things quickly got out of hand for him. He would borrow money and charge up his credit cards to the limit to support his habit. When he ran into serious financial trouble, he began engaging in fraudulent activity to fund his habit.

Relationships with Brad's loved ones deteriorated over time. His family and friends could no longer rely on him since he would disappear for days at a time to gamble. He ran up more and more debt until he was discovered and accused of fraud. Brad received an eight-year prison term.

Brad experienced profound disorientation and isolation while incarcerated. He felt terrible about the harm he had caused to his loved ones, and he had lost all that was important to him. The jail chaplain, however, became a source of comfort as he listened to his confessions and guided him away from his destructive path.

Brad realized that his actions had affected others not just monetarily, but also psychologically. He started confronting his gambling and substance abuse problems and accepting responsibility for them. He was slowly reassembling the shattered person he once was.

Brad had changed dramatically by the time he finished his sentence. He discovered new meaning in his life by assisting others going through the same difficulties he had. After serving his sentence, he promised himself he would return to his loved ones as a changed man.

Brad didn't give up until he had won their love and forgiveness again. He proved to them that he had turned his life around and began mending the bridges that his addiction and dishonesty had torn apart. The road to redemption was long and winding for Brad, but he finally arrived at the realization that it is never too late to improve himself.

Brad's story is an inspiring account of redemption and personal growth. Brad was a man who seemed to have it all, but he was doomed by his gambling habit. He was suddenly locked up and saw no way out of his predicament. However, the path he followed while behind bars gave him faith in his ability to change and redeem himself.

When you've changed for the better, it's time to let people who were hurt by your past actions know about it. Brad understood that he and the people around him had been hurt by his previous choices. He admitted his wrongdoing and made efforts to overcome his addiction and start over. Brad's path to self-improvement was fraught with difficulties and obstacles. But he stuck it out, and he came out of prison a new person.

Brad's rehabilitation involved more than just abandoning his gambling habit. In addition, he had to face his failures of the past head-on and accept responsibility for them. Brad had to face the reality that his actions had resulted in suffering for other people. He needed to practice self-forgiveness and ask for others' forgiveness. Through introspection and development, Brad was able to forge a new identity as someone who had triumphed over his past.

Everyone can change for the better after hearing Brad's tale. No matter how far we've gone in the wrong direction, we can always backtrack and begin again. Taking charge of our lives and making an effort to improve ourselves is crucial. To heal ourselves and those around us, it can be helpful to introduce ourselves as new people. It's a method to show the world that we've grown from our experiences and are ready to make a change for the better.

Finally, Brad's life provides a compelling example of the possibility of change. We can always find our way back to ourselves, no matter how disoriented we might currently feel. We can reintroduce ourselves as new people if we accept responsibility for our past mistakes and make a commitment to our development. This is not just the way to recovery, but also the method to encourage others to find their path to wholeness.

7 Ways To Reinvent Yourself
Towards the Path Of Healing

It's no secret that life can be difficult, and that there may be times when it seems like the pain will never end. Fortunately, there are numerous options for reclaiming power and starting over on the road to recovery.

First, determine what it is you want to accomplish in your healing process. Whether you're trying to mend a broken friendship, recover from a terrible experience, or restore your physical and mental health, you'll do better if you set concrete, attainable objectives.

Second, Reach out to those who have been where you are now; talking to those who have been there before can be a huge comfort. They might be able to relate to what you're going through from their own experiences and offer helpful advices as a result.

Third, keep your attention on the things you can change, as it's simple to feel helpless in the face of so many variables over which you have little sway. If you find yourself dwelling on the negative, try shifting your attention to the positive.

Fourth, creating regular time for healthy activities like exercise, meditation, or focusing on a passion can help you maintain a sense of calm and serenity even when life is chaotic. These pursuits might also serve as a welcome diversion from the m stressful internal monologue.

Fifth, it's never too late to visit a therapist, talk to a psychologist, or rely on the support of medical professionals. 5. Seek Professional Help It's never too late to see a therapist, talk to a psychologist, or rely on the support of medical workers. It's important to get help when you need it, and if that means consulting a mental health expert, don't be shy about doing so.

Sixth, it's okay to make mistakes and fail on the way to recovery, so give yourself a break. If you make a mistake and then admit it, take responsibility for it, learn from it, and move on, that's fine. To speed up the healing process, it's important to surround yourself with positive people as much as possible.

Seventh, spend time with supportive friends and family. In addition, use this time to prioritize self-care and include practicing daily life that increases feelings of positivity and loves for yourself.

The process of self-reinvention on the road to recovery may be long and laborious, but you can get a head start by using the seven suggestions provided above.

Activity

Art has the potential to be a potent medium for introspection and restoration. Here's something fun to do:

1. Go somewhere peaceful and relaxing where you may concentrate on your ideas in peace. This exercise can be done with a therapist or a close friend.

2. Before beginning, consider your goals for this endeavor. To what end do you seek to benefit? How do you hope to feel after it's all said and done?

3. Pick an art form that speaks to you, be it painting, drawing, or collage. Get together everything you'll need.

4. Sketch a mental picture of who you are now. Don't stress out over creating a flawless product. Use it to express how you're feeling right now.

5. Now, reflect on the parts of yourself you'd like to change. You can aspire to improve your self-assurance, empathy, or imagination. Start incorporating them into your work. You might use words, colors, or icons to symbolize these characteristics.

6. As you keep creating art, think about the alterations you'd like to make in your life. How can you incorporate these alterations into your regular activities and interpersonal connections?

7. once you've finished your piece of art and are satisfied with it, step back and evaluate it. Is there something about that that reveals something about you? In what ways have you evolved? How can you proceed down the road to recovery and development?

Keep in mind that the point of this exercise is to let your imagination and instincts lead the way. Don't stress about perfection or following the guidelines. Give yourself permission to go off and find out for yourself what is in wait.

Write your journal!

(Write your learning on the 9th Step Towards the Path Of Healing using the space provided with the direction based on the theme given below)

Step 10

Regaining my power

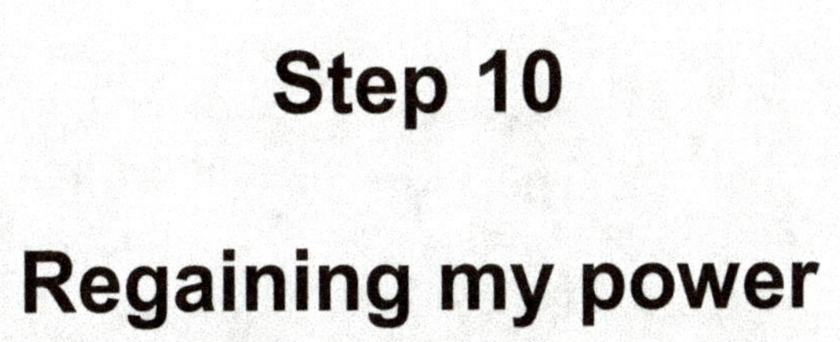

"Like water on a lotus leaf, harmful energy, emotions, and habits can be removed through restorative healing with little to no lasting impact, much like the smooth surface of the lotus leaf. Similar to the lotus leaf's ability to purify itself, restorative healing can help us purge our mental, emotional, and spiritual clutter. The lotus flower is also a symbol of rebirth and rejuvenation because of its close association with enlightenment and spiritual development."

Trike was a brilliant student from the start. However, he feared his world had come to an end after receiving a failing grade in mathematics. The school principal heard his pleas for a second opportunity and reconsidered. The principal, to his astonishment, consented, but with a catch. The teacher had an exchange request for Trike.

What happened next was a terrifying ordeal that left an indelible mark on Trike's mind. The principal sexually assaulted him, and to make matters worse, the incident was caught on camera. The video quickly went viral, and Trike was the target of his classmates' scorn and embarrassment.

Trike was overwhelmed by the incident and unable to recover. His connections suffered as he became more irritable and distant. He even started physically and sexually abusing his partner.

Trike's wife finally snapped one day. With tears in her eyes, she implored him to go get help. For Trike, it was an "aha!" moment. Suddenly, he saw that he was not the only one in need of assistance. Trike saw the need to address the widespread acceptance of sexual abuse of boys and young men and took action to address the issue.

He and his wife decided to see a therapist. Trike worked on his problems for a while and started making headway. He began to share his thoughts and feelings and make efforts to repair his connections.

Trike has evolved into a new person. He is now a prominent voice in the fight to protect young men from sexual predators. He now has something to live for, and his broken bonds with family and friends have been repaired.

If you're feeling broken, take heart from Trike's narrative; repair is possible. Healing is always within grasp, with the correct amount of assistance and encouragement.

The healing process depicted in Trike's narrative is inspiring. He had trouble coping with the aftereffects of a horrific experience and wound up hurting himself and the people he cared about. But he worked up the nerve to get help, and his life has taken a surprising turn for the better ever since.

Real recovery is a process that calls for patience and persistence. It takes courage to take the initial step toward getting help after experiencing the grief and trauma that may be holding us back. Trike's wife pushed him to see a doctor, but there are alternative options like counseling and support groups he could have used instead.

Getting to the bottom of what's causing us pain is a crucial part of any process of restoration. The sexual assault Trike endured changed his life and his outlook in significant ways. However, he was able to start healing and rebuilding his life after confronting this tragedy and working through his pain.

It's also crucial to understand how our activities affect the people in our immediate vicinity. The hurt Trike felt from his own experience led directly to his abusive behavior towards his partner. After he started working on himself, though, he was able to mend his relationships and rediscover his sense of purpose.

Last but not least, Trike's narrative stresses the significance of lending a hand to those in need. By speaking out against the sexual abuse of young men, he has been able to leverage his own horrific experiences to effect positive change in the world.

We can heal from our wounds if we are brave enough to face them, reach out for support, and draw wisdom from our experiences to share with others. There is always hope for a better tomorrow, and Trike's story is a powerful reminder of that no matter how devastated we feel today.

FREE QUAN
R.I.P
Mama

7 Methods To Bounce Back and Restore Healing from Emotional Setback

The distressing thoughts and feelings associated with a traumatic event might be challenging to forget. However, overcoming trauma and the negative emotions it causes is essential to recovery. Here are seven ways that people who have experienced trauma might learn to heal and go on with their lives.

1. Seek Outside Assistance First. Going to therapy can be a very beneficial step toward processing and coping with prior trauma. Working with a skilled expert can help you establish healthy coping mechanisms and learn techniques for managing challenging emotions.

2. Engage in Mindful Activity. To practice mindfulness, one must bring one's full, undivided attention to whatever is happening right now without passing judgment on anything. To shield yourself from the invasive thoughts of the past, practice living in the here and now.

3. Share Some of your Personal Stories. The first step in recovery from trauma is finding safe people to talk to about it. Despite the stigma associated with discussing traumatic experiences, doing so can be beneficial for both the individual and the community as a whole.

4. Work Out. If you're looking for a healthy alternative to destructive coping techniques like substance misuse or self-harm, then make time for regular physical activity. Working out is a terrific method to release any pent-up fury healthily.

5. Make a Note of It. Writing about painful experiences and the feelings that came along with emitting can be therapeutic for some people. Similar to talking to a therapist, writing can help you sort through and release bad emotions and thoughts.

6. Put Limits in Place. Protecting yourself by putting distance between yourself and people, places, or things that can bring up unpleasant emotions or memories is a good strategy for maintaining composure under pressure.

7. Make Self-care a Top Priority. Recognizing and meeting one's own needs is a crucial first step on the road to recovery. Putting yourself first and making sure you get the rest, relaxation, or whatever you need that day. This can contribute to a feeling of security and well-being, both of which are important for the healing process.

Using these strategies, trauma survivors can strengthen their ability to bounce back from adversity and regain control of their lives. Although it may take some time, you can overcome the effects of trauma and get your life back on track if you put in the effort.

Activity

LOVE CUPS VS. ANGER CUPS

What you'll need:
Five cups, Ten marbles, Pen

Steps:

First, assign each cup a distinct feeling, like "angry," "fearful," "sad," "guilty," or "ashamed."

The second step is to get a different cup and put the marbles in there. Your suppressed feelings will be represented by these pebbles.

Third, label each cup with an emotion, then use the pen to jot down the exact events or situations that triggered those feelings.

Fourth, take a marble from the cup, and that feeling will be the one you focus on for the next few days.

Fifth, say the emotion aloud while holding the marble. Recognize the feeling and the circumstances surrounding it. Pause for a while and think about how you feel.

Sixth, Put the "anger" marble, for example, in the "love" cup. Move the marble to the cup that represents the opposing emotion.

Seventh, Do the same thing again, but this time with the opposite feeling in mind, and this time use a different cup.

Eight, Take a deep breath and evaluate how you feel after putting the marbles in their respective cups. Do you feel like a weight has been lifted and your emotions have changed?

Ninth, think about what you learned from the exercise and how you can utilize it in the future to let out pent-up feelings.

Feelings related to past traumas can be processed and released through this exercise. It might help you replace your bad feelings with happier ones. It can be done independently or with the help of a therapist or other trusted person.

Write your journal!

(Write your learning on the 10th Step Towards the Path Of Healing using the space provided with the direction based on the theme given below)

"Regaining Your Power: Overcoming Past Hurts and Moving Forward"

Afterword

The road to recovery from wounds like abandonment, abuse, and pain is not a smooth one. You'll need strength, courage, determination, and a healthy dose of self-love to make it. It's a road that requires us to confront our worst anxieties, hurts, and wounds. But it's also a way to personal development and independence.

It's possible that we'll all have to go through some tough times in our lives. Anxiety, sadness, and post-traumatic stress disorder are just a few examples of the emotional and mental health problems we may face. Past relationships, traumatic experiences as children, and cultural and institutional oppression can all leave scars on us. We could feel abandoned, despondent, and powerless.

However, there is still a chance. It is possible to heal. It's possible; it just might require some time, energy, and help. We have the ability to train ourselves to develop resiliency, self-compassion, and positive coping mechanisms. We have the option to seek out healing through talk therapy, support groups, or other methods like yoga, meditation, or the arts. In community, we can discover acceptance, understanding, and support from those who have been where we have been.

The purpose of this book is to examine the process of recovering from traumas including abuse, neglect, and emotional wounds. Individuals who have already set out on this path will speak to us, imparting their experiences, thoughts, and advice. We will gain an understanding of the healing process, from recognizing and accepting our suffering to working through and letting go of our feelings to finally integrating and growing beyond them. On our travels, we will also learn the value of self-love, self-acceptance, and self-determination.

I wish you peace and healing, and I pray that this book will help you along the way. I hope you find the strength and community you need to overcome obstacles and make the most of chances for personal development and positive change. Be reminded that you deserve kindness, reverence, and restoration. Wishing you the comfort of knowing you are not alone.

References:

- Specifically: Brown, B. The strength in being exposed [TEDTalk]. Get this talk by Brené Brown on vulnerability at https://www.ted.com/talks?language=en.

- D. J. Siegel (2010). Mindsight is cutting-edge research on changing one's mind. Bantam Books, New York.

  In I. Yalom & S. A. Perennial Classics: Love's Executioner and Other Stories of Psychotherapy. Published by Perennial in the Big Apple.

ABOUT THE AUTHOR

I am **Marquis Dorsey**. Who has been shattered by past trauma, I felt like I was screaming, but no one could hear me. My anguish fell on deaf ears, so I used it as motivation and transformed it into strength. Knowing that I was the only member of my family who had never been incarcerated gave me power.

From my mother's substance abuse and prioritization of drugs over her children to my molestation at the hands of a new roommate, my life has been riddled with tragedy.

I wanted to prove to the world that I could overcome adversity and succeed according to my standards. I measure my success based on who I was the day before, not the success of others. I carried it on my sleeve that I was the youngest member of my family and the first to graduate, giving my mother something to be proud of. As soon as I realized what the issue was, I made sure it was resolved.

Three words would suffice to characterize me:

Resilient, Resolute, and Brave.

I'm built to withstand any environment, and I'm proud to be from Detroit and to have made it this far.